LONDON

A VIEW FROM THE STREETS

LONDON

A VIEW FROM THE STREETS

ANNA MAUDE

THE BRITISH MUSEUM PRESS

Contents

Introduction   6

Celebration   10

Eating and drinking   20

Shopping   36

Pleasure   50

Traffic and transport   70

Construction   84

Fire, crime and punishment   96

Further reading   112

Introduction

IN THE TWO CENTURIES BETWEEN the Great Fire of 1666 and the Great Exhibition of 1851, London transformed beyond all recognition. The rebuilding of the city following the fire was only the beginning of a remarkable phase of urban history. The eighteenth century saw the emergence of the West End as a smart residential quarter, built around elegant squares. As the century progressed, so did the city; marching inexorably onwards to the surrounding villages of Hampstead, Highgate and Knightsbridge. The pace of urbanization again increased at the dawn of the nineteenth century, with the advent of the industrial revolution and an explosion in the population. By 1851, the date of the Great Exhibition, London stood proudly as the largest, most influential city in the world, dazzling foreigners and eliciting praise from social commentators. Never before in history has one city witnessed such dramatic transformation as London in the nineteenth century, yet this fascinating subject has been largely shunned by the major artists of the time. It was not until the latter decades of the nineteenth century, when Impressionists adopted London as a subject, that the city found its place in mainstream art, albeit for its evocative fog rather than the realities of contemporary London life. For a picture of London as perceived by Londoners, one must look instead to the topographers (who depicted views accurately in great graphic detail), satirists and lower echelons of the print trade, whose lively and prolific output provide a charming and richly varied image of life on the streets of London. Their picturing of London in the period sheds light on the issues and constraints that shaped London's visual history.

Views and sketches of the city were largely a reflection of the London people wanted to see. What this might be varied depending on the audience, time and type of image. For the most part London's growth and power were celebrated, particularly by topographers. The magnificence of London was its selling point, and artists capitalized on this, producing views focusing on the grandeur and nobility of the streets and buildings. For the first half of the eighteenth century, the city shown in London topography was a far cry from the city witnessed by Londoners. Bird's-eye views or carefully delineated architectural elevations were the order of the day. This all changed in 1746, with the arrival of the Venetian artist Canaletto (1697–1768) in London. Canaletto's style of topography was a much closer reflection of what people actually see as they walk around a city, and his influence brought the 'view' of London down to the streets. Suddenly perspectives were shifted to eye-level, making views immediately easier to relate to, and street life was introduced, helping to set scale and add realism. That is not to say that views became an accurate reflection of life on the streets as traffic, crime, dirt and bad weather are eradicated from the eighteenth-century vision of London. Most views present well-dressed pedestrians strutting elegantly down wide, spacious streets; the city around them appearing noble, sedate and aloof. By the nineteenth century, however, views began to revel in London's physical expansion; the commerce and industry that had helped London achieve its status were celebrated in busy and industrious street scenes. The series *London as it is* from 1842, by the English artist Thomas Shotter Boys (1803–74), perfectly exemplifies this shift. The views depicted in Boys' series of prints introduce a lively and realistic street life, with street traders, wagons, carriages and coaches mixing with the pedestrians hastily traversing the city. In Boys' London the city is not diminished by the inclusion of its inhabitants, but rather rises above the street life to stamp its authority on the view. Together, the impression is of a flourishing, powerful metropolis, enjoying its success.

One of the limitations of views of London is that they do not acknowledge the contrasts that form the realities of urban living. Extreme wealth and poverty, architectural innovation and slums, and deprivation and power all lived together in the jumbled complexity of city life. Fortunately topographers were not the only artists recording the city. Graphic satirists were also busily putting pen to paper in an attempt to capture the life around them. Focusing on London's inhabitants rather than architecture, sketches considered the life of the city. The most prolific producers of sketches of London life were the satirists, notably William Hogarth (1697–1764), George Cruikshank

(1792–1878) and Thomas Rowlandson (1756–1827). Their work was designed to present London to Londoners, and often played on local knowledge for full effect. Satire was often designed for the lower classes, either through satirical observations of the high-life or, more commonly, in the colourful characterizations of the poor, and so these prints provide a light-hearted picture of London society. They are especially interesting when illuminating the habits and customs of London's low-life, as topographers avoided the subject, or imposed picturesque qualities on their representations of the poor. In addition to the satirists were draughtsmen such as George Scharf (1788–1860), who seemed to delight in sketching ordinary London life, for its own sake. Active in the first half of the nineteenth century, Scharf carefully sketched hundreds of London street scenes, and took particular care to record any signs of change and modernization. Most of these sketches were not designed for sale, but were produced purely to satisfy the artist's own interest in London's streets. The large collection of Scharf's sketches in the British Museum's collection provide a unique glimpse into the commonplace activities of Londoners at a time of striking change in the city. In the latter half of the nineteenth century, sketches and satires grew darker as the glow of London's modernization began to fade, and the resultant crime, poverty and disease became more apparent. Gustav Doré's (1832–1883) famous illustrations to *London: A Pilgrimage* (1872) are a case in point. However, in the period covered by this book, London was still coming to terms with its monumental growth and success, and little time was spent dwelling on the darker implications.

The British Museum is fortunate to have a wealth of visual material on London, though much of it is largely unknown, bound up in albums and portfolios across the Museum's collection. Drawing on the diversity of the Museum's expansive London collection, this book brings together a selection of fascinating images to explore a number of themes related to the everyday life of Londoners, on all levels of society. The matter of living in London, with all the ordinariness, tedium, wonder and pleasure that urban life entails, has intrigued draughtsmen and printmakers, and luckily for us there were some who made it their business to record what they saw. The city as an entity was changing and growing so dramatically, and at such a pace, that many had to look closer to make sense of what was happening; to the streets they lived on and the activities of their neighbours. While London was busily engorging the countryside and polluting its rivers, Rowlandson was more distracted by the traffic, describing with a typically sharp eye the ruckus caused by clashing carriages and construction on a narrow street in his *Miseries of London* prints. The fact that grand new bridges were being built over the River Thames did not stop Isaac Cruikshank (1756–1811) from illustrating the peculiar, parochial tradition of 'swearing on the horns' at a tavern in Highgate. James McNeill Whistler (1834–1903) chose to illustrate fish shops in Chelsea rather than the looming improvements, while others delighted in the new and modern. Rag Fair and Regent Street have both found their place, as have the Beggar's Opera and banquets in Guildhall. Fireworks, executions, taverns and zoos were all part of life in London, and all have made their way into the image of the city left to posterity. London was teaming with life and energy, some of it elegant and prosperous, other parts grubby and depraved; all of it captivating. This is exemplified in a poem prefacing Francis Newbery's 1775 edition of *The Cries of London*, which sums up the extraordinary range and vitality of the metropolis:

> *Houses, churches, mix'd together,*
> *Streets unpleasant in all weather;*
> *Prisons, palaces, and shops,*
> *Courts of justice, fatal drops;*
> *Exhibitions, masquerades,*
> *Bridges bright — grand arcades,*
> *Pipers, fiddlers tumblers, harpers,*
> *Puppets, pickpockets, and sharpers;*
> *Tipsy barrow-women tumbling,*
> *Dukes and chimney-sweepers jumbling:*
> *Chairmen, Carmen, kennel-rakers,*
> *Catchpoles, bailiffs, and thief-takers;*
> *Many a bargain, could ye strike it*
> *This is London. How d'ye like it?*

Celebration

LONDON HAS NEVER BEEN SHY of a good celebration, and the city has witnessed some spectacular public events, often at great expense. The narrowness of city streets and the residential status of the squares meant that the most impressive celebrations took place on the River Thames, or in the parks. Flotillas down the Thames for the Lord Mayor's Procession were famously captured by Canaletto in the mid eighteenth century; his views benefiting from the recently constructed Westminster Bridge, opened in 1750. Unlike today, spectators were not sidelined to the riverbank, as many watched from the plentiful small boats and barges lining the river. Parks were the preferred location for grand firework displays, often involving the construction of an extravagant temporary structure. The expense of such an occasion was a mark of the city's affluence, and while celebrations were always in the name of a particular event, they can also be seen as celebrations of London itself.

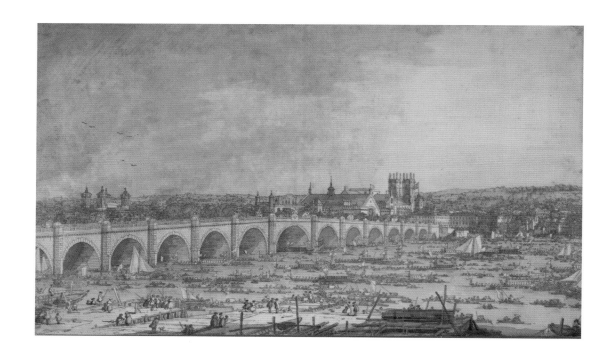

Westminster Bridge

PEN AND BROWN INK
WITH GREY WASH, *c.*1750,
BY ANTONIO CANALETTO
(1697–1768)

30.7 x 51.7 cm. British Museum,
1857,0520.61.

Swearing an oath to the monarch is a requirement of all newly elected Lord Mayors of London, and the occasion is marked by a procession through the city and, up until 1856, by a flotilla along the River Thames to Westminster Hall. Canaletto here shows us the splendid mass of boats passing Westminster Bridge, with the Houses of Parliament and Westminster Abbey in the background.

A Perfect Description of the Firework in Covent Garden

that was performed at the charge of the gentry and other inhabitants of that parish for the joyfull return of his majestie from his conquest in Ireland, Sept. 10 1690

Extravagant firework displays such as this were generally reserved for the celebration of military victories and peace treaties, in this case the king's successful campaign in the Jacobite War in Ireland (1689–91). This lively mezzotint shows Covent Garden piazza at night; the glow of the fireworks illuminating St Paul's Church to the right and revellers in the square. In 1690 Inigo Jones's Covent Garden piazza was an elegant, well-respected residential quarter, and its inhabitants were among London's elite. As the eighteenth century progressed its reputation declined, with the busy market attracting a more bohemian crowd, tolerant of the noise and mess.

MEZZOTINT, 1690, BY BERNARD LENS II (1659–1725)

34.7 x 26.7 cm. British Museum, 1853,0813.103.

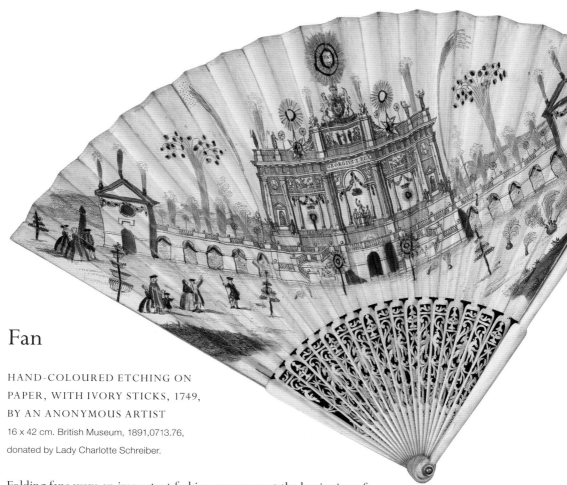

Fan

HAND-COLOURED ETCHING ON
PAPER, WITH IVORY STICKS, 1749,
BY AN ANONYMOUS ARTIST

16 x 42 cm. British Museum, 1891,0713.76,
donated by Lady Charlotte Schreiber.

Folding fans were an important fashion accessory at the beginning of
the eighteenth century, and by the 1720s, large numbers were being
printed for sale. Although many were simply decorative, publishers
would use well-known prints or satires on particular political events
tailored to particular audiences. The fan here is a souvenir of the
Royal Fireworks that took place in 1749, in celebration of the peace
of Aix-la-Chapelle. It depicts the temporary buildings erected in
Green Park, where the firework display was held.

Trade card

of Samuel Clanfield, firework engineer, at the
Royal Fireworks in Hosier Lane, West Smithfield

ETCHING WITH ENGRAVED LETTERING,
*c.*1750, BY AN ANONYMOUS ARTIST

16.7 x 23.7 cm. British Museum, Heal, 62.4 cm.

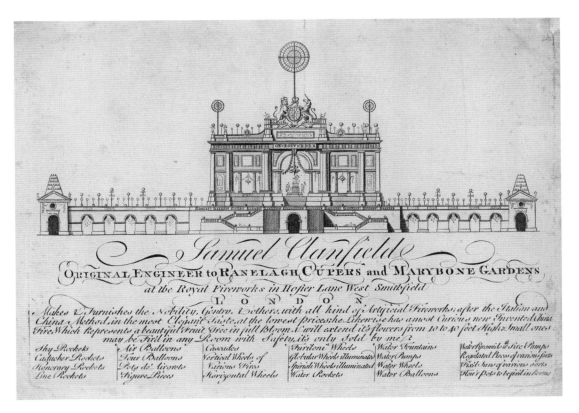

Samuel Clanfield

ORIGINAL ENGINEER to RANELAGH CUPERS and MARYBONE GARDENS

at the Royal Fireworks in Hosier Lane West Smithfield

LONDON

Makes & furnishes the Nobility, Gentry, & others, with all kind of Artificial Fireworks, after the Italian and China Method, in the most Elegant Taste, at the lowest prices, he Likewise has a most Curious new Invented China Fire, Which Represents a beautiful Fruit Tree in full Bloom, & will extend it's flowers from 10 to 40 feet High & small ones may be Fir'd in any Room with Safety, it's only Sold by me.

Sky Rockets	Air Balloons	Cascades	Spiritoni Wheels	Water Fountains	Water Plynmills & Fire Pumps
Caducher Rockets	Four Balloons	Vertical Wheels of	Globular Wheels illuminated	Water Pumps	Regulated Pieces of various forts
Honorary Rockets	Pots de Airoets	Various Fires	Spiritil Wheels illuminated	Water Wheels	Frost Suns of various sorts
Line Rockets	Figure Pieces	Horizontal Wheels	Water Rockets	Water Balloons	Flour Pots to be fir'd in Rooms

The Opening of New London Bridge

by their most gracious majesties
William the 4th & Queen Adelaide

For many years London Bridge stood as the only land route over the River Thames, a vital point of connection between Southwark and the City. However, its medieval origins ensured that by the early nineteenth century this well-trodden bridge desperately needed replacement. The new bridge was opened in 1831, and Havell's print shows the pageantry involved in the event as decorative and ceremonial barges, boats and steamships carpet the river, flags line the bridge, and a hot-air balloon tops the occasion.

ETCHING AND AQUATINT
WITH HAND-COLOURING,
1831, BY ROBERT HAVELL II
(1793–1878)
28.1 x 43.3 cm. British Museum,
1880,1113.1592.

The Chinese Bridge Illuminated

Dubourg's print is another example of the elaborate celebrations put on in the capital in the name of military achievement. In this instance an entire bridge and pagoda have been built in St James's Park as a platform for fireworks celebrating the 1814 Treaty of Paris, which ended the Napoleonic Wars.

ETCHING AND AQUATINT WITH HAND-COLOURING, 1814, BY MATTHEW DUBOURG (1806–1838 *fl.*)

18.3 x 24.9 cm. British Museum, 1880,1113.2375.

Opening of Hungerford Market

In a time before the convenience of the deep freeze and cargo planes, markets were a vital source of fresh food for London's inhabitants. As the population of the city exploded in the nineteenth century, markets needed to increase capacity, or risk being overrun. Miles's drawing captures the opening of the new Hungerford Market on the River Thames – an elegant and capacious structure replacing a ramshackle collection of sheds and low buildings. Primarily a fish market, space was also built for fresh fruit, vegetables and meat, and facilities were provided for the docking of steamships on the Thames front. Despite this, the market was unsuccessful, and was demolished in 1862 to make way for Charing Cross Station.

WATERCOLOUR, 1833, BY G. H. MILES (1824–1840 *fl.*)

21.9 x 26.2 cm. British Museum, 1880,1113.1385.

Eating and drinking

EVERYONE NEEDS TO EAT, and a city as large as London provided a wide range of social and public situations for doing so. From banquets to stalls, the city catered for all occasions. If it was just food Londoners were after, the city would have been a very different place! Taverns and gin houses littered certain quarters, and the problems caused by the cheap availability of gin sparked a whole movement of moral reformers in Victorian London. Alcohol of course did not only affect the poor, and in the eighteenth century it – particularly the impact of excessive drinking and a debauched lifestyle of London's rakes – was a popular subject among satirists, most famously William Hogarth in his series of *Modern Moral Subjects*. Artists have tackled the subject from many different angles over the period, providing a rich and diverse selection of images detailing how London's population fed and lubricated itself in public.

BEER STREET.

Beer, happy Produce of our Isle
Can sinewy Strength impart,
And wearied with Fatigue and Toil
Can cheer each manly Heart.

Labour and Art upheld by Thee
Successfully advance,
We quaff Thy balmy Juice with Glee
And Water leave to France.

Genius of Health, thy grateful Taste
Rivals the Cup of Jove,
And warms each English generous Breast
With Liberty and Love.

Price 1.ʳ

Design'd by W. Hogarth.   Publish'd according to Act of Parliament Feb. 1 1751.

Beer Street and Gin Lane

Beer Street (left) serves as a pair to *Gin Lane* (shown right) and is intended as a celebration of the benefits of drinking beer compared with the destructive effects of gin. In *Beer Street* Hogarth shows us a jolly company enjoying beer from tankards on the streets outside a tavern. They are well fed and good humoured – in stark contrast to the emaciated figures in *Gin Lane* – toasting the king on his birthday. Social gatherings in London's taverns and inns were a major part of life for many Londoners, and Hogarth here reminds us that not all drinking patterns among the lower classes were morally reprehensible.

Left and above ETCHING AND ENGRAVINGS, 1751, BY WILLIAM HOGARTH (1697–1764)
37.8 x 32.3 cm and 38.5 x 32 cm.
British Museum, 1868,0822.1594 and 1868,0822.1595, both bequeathed by Felix Slade.

GIN LANE.

The Covt: Garden Morning Frolick

This print highlights the decline of Covent Garden by the mid eighteenth century. Here Boitard lightly satirizes the less than dignified outcome of a night of drunkenness for three well-dressed companions, making their way home in the early hours through the market.

ETCHING, 1747, BY
LOUIS PHILIPPE BOITARD
(1733–1767 *fl.*)
24.5 x 32.2 cm. British Museum,
1860,0623.29.

Invented by Wm. Hogarth.

A COUNTRY INN YARD AT THE TIME O

ELECTION.

J. June Sculp.

A Country Inn Yard at the Time of an Election

Long distance road travel by coach required numerous inns on route for refreshing horses and travellers alike. Inns were therefore based around a galleried courtyard, where passengers loaded up for travel, and horses were attended to. June's print shows a coach being loaded up in the courtyard of the 'Old Angel Inn'. The railway changed all this, forcing inns and taverns to reinvent themselves, which they did with vigour in the nineteenth century. Large decorative windows, inviting twinkling lights, and dressed up bars presented an attractive façade, drawing in passing trade. This remains the blueprint of pub design today.

ETCHING AND ENGRAVING, 1750–70,
BY JOHN JUNE (1744–1775 *fl.*), AFTER
WILLIAM HOGARTH (1697–1764)
24.9 x 35.2 cm. British Museum, 1871,1209.2817.

A Scene at the Beggar's Opera in St Giles's

A group of people sitting down to a meal in the Beggar's Opera, located in the notorious slum of St Giles. Cruikshank does not shy away from the poverty of the scene, but by choosing to represent people tucking into a healthy meal, he shows us a moment of relative comfort. Most representations of poverty set out to shock or moralize, but here Cruikshank simply observes, albeit with an element of satirical flourish.

Tankard

STONEWARE TANKARD DEPICTING THREE KINGS IN RENAISSANCE COURT DRESS. MADE IN GERMANY, *c.*1531–40, FOUND IN LONDON

H. 12.2 cm. British Museum, 1895,0116.8, donated by Sir Augustus Wollaston Franks.

THE BEGGAR'S OPERA" *in S.ͭGiles's.— Sketched on the Spot.*

ETCHING AND AQUATINT,
1822, BY GEORGE
CRUIKSHANK (1792–1878).
13.7 x 22.6 cm. British Museum,
1937,0729.77.

A View of the inside of Guildhall

as it appear'd on Lord Mayor's Day, 1761

Banquets such as this provided an opportunity to reassert hierarchy and authority. The seating plan would have been carefully judged, and the expense of the occasion highlighted the resources and affluence of the Lord Mayor of London.

ETCHING, 1761, BY
AN ANONYMOUS ARTIST
18.6 x 22.9 cm. British Museum,
G,11.154, bequeathed by
John Charles Crowle.

Chas Ansell Del.^t   Geo. Townly Stubbs Sculp.

Refreshment at St Giles's

The simple interior of this gin house is typical for the time.
People did not go out to drink gin for the setting, but to
get drunk, and the cheapness of the spirit made this all too
achievable. Makeshift dram-shops, such as the one pictured
here, were set up in many households in London's rougher
areas in the mid eighteenth century.

ETCHING AND STIPPLE
WITH HAND-COLOURING,
1789, BY GEORGE TOWNLEY
STUBBS (1748–1815), AFTER
CHARLES ANSELL (1784–96 *fl.*)
23 x 24.4 cm. British Museum,
1948,0315.6.36, bequeathed by
Hermann Marx.

The Devil Reproving Sin

From 1760 to 1800 Bagnigge Wells was one of the most popular
and fashionable spas in London. The discovery of iron rich waters
in the garden led to its foundation as a spa and tea room, with
gardens stretching on to the Fleet River. However, by 1800 the
wells were attracting a lower class of customer, and so the
fashionable crowd went elsewhere. This print shows the wells
after this turn; the leering face of the waiter hinting at the less
reputable nature of his customers.

HAND-COLOURED
ETCHING, 1804, BY AN
ANONYMOUS ARTIST
19.8 x 24.6 cm. British Museum,
1985,0119.200.

Tea Garden at Jack Straw's Castle

Tea gardens attached to taverns in the suburbs were popular places for refreshment and social meetings for London's more refined inhabitants. Scharf's drawing shows us the tea garden at the back of Jack Straw's Castle, a well-known coaching inn in Hampstead frequented by Charles Dickens, among other London characters.

Above BRUSH DRAWING IN GREY WASH, 1830, BY GEORGE SCHARF (1788–1860)
12.7 x 22.1 cm. British Museum, 1862,0614.693.

WHITE METAL ADMISSION-TICKET FOR THE ST HELENA TAVERN AND TEA GARDENS, IN ROTHERHITHE, LONDON. DATE UNCERTAIN
Diam. 3.9 cm. British Museum, MG.760, donated by Montague Guest.

Swearing at Highgate

The practice of 'Swearing on the Horns' was a ritual encouraging debauched and promiscuous behaviour – first begun at a tavern in Highgate, north London – whereby regular customers would do their best to convince newcomers to confirm their dedication to making merry by swearing on the horns. In this print Cruikshank shows the ritual being performed on a clueless countryman, who is accosted by the landlord and said horns at the entrance to the tavern. His confusion elicits much merriment among the other tavern goers.

ETCHING WITH HAND-COLOURING, 1796,
BY ISAAC CRUIKSHANK (1756–1811), AFTER
GEORGE MOUTARD WOODWARD (*c.*1760–1809)

17.6 x 21.1 cm. British Museum, 1927,1126.1.9.3, bequeathed by George Potter.

The Great Social Evil

This print shows a meeting in St James's Hall, put on by philanthropic and well-meaning ladies and gentleman, with the aim of convincing 'unfortunate females' to give up their life of degradation, and accept their offer of reforming 'homes'. Many of the ladies present have attended for the free tea and cake, indicating the power of food to bring people together. This print is an example of the growing desire for social reform among some sections of Victorian society.

HAND-COLOURED
LITHOGRAPH, *c.*1850, BY
AN ANONYMOUS ARTIST
25.2 x 39 cm. British Museum,
2002,U.270.

Shopping

SHOPPING IN LONDON was a starkly contrasting experience for rich and poor. For those living in slums or small, crowded city dwellings, shopping meant food and basics, such as matches and kindling. These did not come from a building with walls, but from the markets and street traders that thronged the streets. The rich had servants to shop for basics, and for them, shopping was a pastime. Impressive arcades and shopping streets were the domain of the rich, selling luxury goods to those prospering from London's booming economy. The emergence of a luxury retail market in the City and the West End was an eighteenth-century phenomenon, boosting the attractiveness of London as a destination for the elite.

View over Smithfield Market, looking towards Giltspur Street

Up until 1855, Smithfield Market was a cattle market, with livestock brought into the city for slaughter. When it was first formally established in 1638, Smithfield was on the edge of the city, surrounded by open fields. This view shows the market in the nineteenth century, after London had well and truly encompassed the space. The market is in full swing, with traders bartering and examining cattle around pens.

HAND-COLOURED ETCHING AND AQUATINT, 1831, BY RICHARD GILSON REEVE (1803–89), AFTER JAMES POLLARD (1792–1867)
38.6 x 64.7 cm. British Museum, 1880,1113.4157.

Smithfield Market. (*Death of*) *This Print is Pub.ᵈ in* Commemoration of Smit
the **Lord Mayor**. *& Corporation of the City of London. with my b*
hagen-fields & Islington. — N.B. The nighest Police court Clark

Smithfield Market (Death of)

The practicalities of holding a live cattle market in the centre of the city had come under serious scrutiny by the mid nineteenth century. The practice of herding livestock through narrow streets to the market led to frequent stampedes, with animals ending up in shops or houses, spreading dung across the city. Blood from their slaughter created a lingering stench and, in 1855, the decision was made to move the market to Islington. In this print Marks satirizes the chaos of the weekly market, showing a stampeding bull trampling stalls, scattering livestock and throwing men, leaving destruction in its wake.

rket. & Dedicated to the Rt. Hon.
es to the inhabitance of Copen—
!!! J.L.Marks Long Lane Smithfield.

HAND-COLOURED ETCHING, 1852–5,

BY J. LEWIS MARKS (c.1796–1855)

23.5 x 37.8 cm. British Museum, 1927,1126.1.5.12,

bequeathed by George Potter.

Billingsgate

Billingsgate Market is the most famous fish market in the city, built around the principal mooring for fishing vessels in the capital. It was made up of small sheds and booths, with fish sold in the open from large baskets. A rowdy trade was carried out from Billingsgate, and this view is surprising for showing a well-dressed company of women shopping from the stalls. The market was moved to the Isle of Dogs, in the East End of London, in 1982.

ETCHING, 1798, BY CHARLES
ANSELL (1784–96 *fl.*)
41.7 x 51.7 cm. British Museum,
1880,1113.3395.

Old Covent Garden Market

WATERCOLOUR, 1825,
BY GEORGE SCHARF
(1788–1860)

24.8 x 37.9 cm. British Museum,
1862,0614.31.

Covent Garden holds London's most famous market. Originally a scattering of stalls in a smart residential area, the market grew and grew, attracting more trade as surrounding markets closed. In this view Scharf shows us the old market, still based around stalls and wooden shelters. As with many of London's markets, the old layout became too impractical with the growth of the population, and in 1828, Charles Fowler designed the new market, which still stands today.

G Scharf del. 1825. London. Old Covent Garden Market. Frucht und Gemüß Markt in London

Westminster Dairy on Regent Street

For the fashionable shopper, John Nash's Regent Street presented a haven. Lined with smart shops, the pavement was protected from the elements by an elegant colonnade. Completed in 1820, it was but one part of sweeping changes made to the city by Nash in the name of the Prince Regent. Scharf's drawing shows a dairy, glimpsed through two columns of the colonnade, the interior of the shop glowing warmly through its glass frontage.

WATERCOLOUR, 1825,
BY GEORGE SCHARF
(1788–1860)
22.8 x 13.8 cm. British Museum,
1862,0614.122.

Fish Shop, Chelsea

Whistler's views of Chelsea shop fronts were made fifty years after Scharf's London sketches, but they were both inspired by a desire to record a rapidly changing city. By the 1870s, the improvements had reached the west banks of the River Thames, and the shop fronts Whistler records here were soon after destined for demolition.

ETCHING, 1878, BY JAMES MCNEILL WHISTLER (1834–1903)

13.9 X 21.6 cm. British Museum, 1918,1012.5, donated by Ernest C. Innes.

Rag Fair

In sharp contrast to John Nash's Regent Street was the Rag Fair.
Located on Rosemary Lane, near the Tower of London, Rag Fair
was really a market for the poor, specializing in old, cheap clothes.
Much of the produce had, by the time it reached the market, been
reduced to rags after passing through many hands, and goods were
displayed in piles and sacks for customers to peruse. Rowlandson's
view emphasizes the poverty of the scene, with the shop sellers and
customers at points difficult to distinguish from the piles of rags.

WATERCOLOUR, DATE
UNCERTAIN, BY THOMAS
ROWLANDSON (1756–1827)
16.8 x 25.6 cm. British Museum,
1880,1113.3509.

Messrs Harding Howell & Co., 89 Pall Mall

Here, well-dressed customers are shown shopping for luxury fabrics displayed hanging from columns or on large rolls in the elegant, open, spacious drapers. There appears to be a sales assistant on hand for every customer. This was a shop only frequented by the well-off.

HAND-COLOURED ETCHING AND AQUATINT, 1809, BY AN ANONYMOUS ARTIST
15.1 x 23.7 cm. British Museum, Heal, Topography.387, bequeathed by Sir Ambrose Heal.

Street traders

For many, street traders were the main source of goods. In these two prints the street traders are placed in identifiable locations, namely St James's Palace and the Mansion House, showing that even the smartest areas were not free from the cries of London.

THE MANSION HOUSE – MATCHES! AND ST JAMES'S PALACE – CHERRIES. HAND-COLOURED ETCHINGS, 1804, AFTER WILLIAM MARSHALL CRAIG (c.1765–1834)
13.1 x 9.8 cm. and 13.1 x 10.2 cm. British Museum, 1948,0315.11.111 and 1948,0315.4.10, both bequeathed by Hermann Marx.

Pleasure

LONDON ABOUNDED WITH OPPORTUNITIES
for leisure and entertainment. In addition to the pleasure gardens
of Vauxhall and Ranelagh, there were fairs, parks, spas, exhibitions,
theatre, concerts, and sports; all designed to entertain the masses.
As mentioned in the previous chapter, shopping emerged as a
pleasurable luxury pastime for the rich, as did promenades through
fashionable London streets and parks. The popularity of spas and
pleasure grounds would flux and wane over the period; their ability
to draw in London's more elegant inhabitants determined their
status. Other forms of pleasure were more spontaneous; frost fairs
on the River Thames, ice-skating, picnics and promenades all
depended on the vagaries of the British weather. Nevertheless,
London's inhabitants were well catered for when it came to
pleasure, with something available for everyone.

FROST FAIR ON THE RIVER THAMES

As it appeared in the hard Frost, Feb'y 4 1814 between London and Blackfriars Bridge when the river was one sheet of Ice and Snow and on which several trades and pastimes were carried on, the above View was taken on that Spot at Bankside Feb'y 4.

Frost Fair on the River Thames

HAND-COLOURED
WOODCUT, 1814, BY AN
ANONYMOUS ARTIST

36.2 x 45 cm. British Museum,
1931,1114.394, donated by
F. Laura Cannan.

In the past, severe frosts could cause the River Thames to freeze over so completely, that fairs were held on the ice. The small arches of the old London Bridge aided the freeze, which was solid enough for booths and stalls to be erected, games to be played, oxen roasted, and even printing presses were brought on the ice to create small souvenir plates. Frost fairs were rare, occurring only in 1683–4, 1715–16, 1739–40, and finally in 1814. After this, the

This view of London Printed on the Ice of the River Thames February 5th 1814

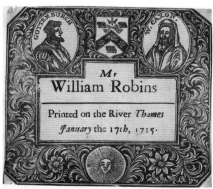

GOTTENBURGH · W. CAXON.

Mr William Robins

Printed on the River *Thames* *January* the 17th, 1715.

rebuilding of London Bridge prohibited a freeze that could support a fair. While canny publishers and booth owners made some money from the event, others lost out – in particular the watermen and fishermen, whose trade ceased for the duration of the frost.

Tickets printed on the Thames

Small tickets or plates were printed on the ice during frost fairs as souvenirs of the occasion. These included portraits and views embellished with personalized letterpress, poems and rhymes on the frost, or simply names and dates, all stating that they were 'Printed on the Thames during the frost Fair…'. The British Museum's collection includes a bound folio of these souvenir plates, which will ensure a selection of these fascinating prints are saved.

Left WOODCUT, 1716; *above* ETCHING, 1814; BOTH BY ANONYMOUS ARTISTS
12.5 x 14.2 cm (left) and 9.1 x 19.3 cm (above).
British Museum, 1880,1113.1785 and 1880,1113.1766.

View of the Garden of the White Conduit House

The White Conduit House was a tavern in Islington that from 1754 offered additional diversions such as cricket, fishing ponds and a tea house. Initially respectable, it became increasingly unruly in the nineteenth century, as shows and fairs were held in the grounds. This view from 1848 shows a tightrope walker entertaining the crowds, who would have also been amused by juggling, farces and ballet. The site was closed and built over in 1849.

PEN AND INK WITH DARK
BROWN WASH, 1848, BY
AN ANONYMOUS ARTIST
11.1 x 15.5 cm. British Museum,
1880,1113.5016.

Chinese Wizard

RICHARDSON

SAU

PIT

J.WALMSLEY.

Bartholomew Fair as it was

Fairs were open to all, and Bartholomew Fair was one of London's largest and most famous fairs. Often raucous and disorderly, fairs also provided rich entertainment, with stage performances and many stalls inducing general merriment. In the nineteenth century the licentious and depraved behaviour of many fair-goers could no longer be ignored, and Bartholomew Fair was eventually closed down in 1855.

WOODCUT, 1841,
BY JOHN WALMSLEY
(1839–78 *fl.*)
20.8 x 33.9 cm. British Museum,
1880,1113.4164.

Drawn by Cruikshanks

Published as the Act directs by W. Locke Sept.r 1.t 1791.

PASTIMES OF PRIMRO

HILL.

Pastimes of Primrose Hill

This print was made before Regent's Park and the surrounding villas were laid out. The hill thus afforded a view over open fields towards the city, making it a popular spot for picnics. It was also more difficult to reach, as Cruikshank's humorous design highlights. A stout man is shown labouring up the hill pulling a pram full of children, his wig has fallen and sits suspended on a pole over his shoulder, while a lady dabs sweat from his forehead. Pleasure, in this instance, is a subjective affair.

ILLUSTRATION TO THE ATTIC
MISCELLANY. ETCHING AND
ENGRAVING, 1791, BY JOHN
BARLOW (1760–1810 *fl.*),
AFTER GEORGE CRUIKSHANK
(1792–1878)
19.2 x 23.2 cm. British Museum,
1880,1113.4690.

THE GREAT INDUSTRIAL EXHIBITIO

Plate 4 The Transept.

1851.

The Great Industrial Exhibition of 1851

The Great Exhibition of 1851 represented the pinnacle of London's success. The many wondrous exhibitions in the Crystal Palace drew in huge crowds marvelling at both the riches on show, and the incredible building housing them. This view of the central transept gives a sense of scale, as a fully grown tree stands at the far end, well under the curved glass ceiling.

COLOUR LITHOGRAPH, 1851,
BY JOSEPH NASH (1808–78)

54.7 x 75.3 cm. British Museum,
1917,1208.2277, donated by Nan Ino
Cooper, Baroness Lucas of Crudwell
and Lady Dingwall.

Admission ticket
for the Great Exhibition of 1851

ENGRAVED IVORY, 1851

Diam. 3.3 cm. British Museum, MG.878,
donated by Montague Guest.

Theatre token

INSCRIBED IVORY TOKEN,
ISSUED BY THEATRE ROYAL
HAYMARKET, 1803

Diam. 3.9 cm. British Museum, MG.167,
donated by Montague Guest.

Theatre interior

Theatre has long been a popular pastime in London, with productions catering for all classes and tastes. From the booth productions of Bartholomew Fair to the plays in the Theatre Royal Drury Lane, theatre flourished in the metropolis. This drawing is a design for a decorative panel for Claridge's Hotel, showing the packed audience and stage of the Theatre Royal Drury Lane as it was in 1800.

PEN AND BROWN INK WITH WATERCOLOUR,
TOUCHED WITH BODYCOLOUR, *c.*1931,
BY GEORGE SHERINGHAM (1884–1937)

42.3 x 51.5 cm. British Museum, 1967,0722.50, donated
by Sheringham Art Trust.

An Inside View of the Rotunda in Ranelagh Gardens

Ranelagh Gardens opened in 1742, as a rival to the pleasure ground at Vauxhall across the River Thames. Ranelagh's main attraction was its rotunda; a large circular building with booths for eating and drinking, a central fireplace, and an orchestra stand. It was brilliantly lit with chandeliers and quickly became London's most fashionable leisure destination. Canaletto made a number of drawings of Ranelagh – this view showing an elegant crowd circulating the interior of the rotunda.

ETCHING WITH HAND-COLOURING AND GRAPHITE, 1751
(THIS STATE 1794),
AFTER ANTONIO
CANALETTO (1697–1768)
26.3 X 40.4 cm. British Museum,
1978,U.3567.

Canaleti delin.

An Inside View of the Rotundo in Ranelagh Gardens

Publish'd according to Act of Parl.

Published 1st May 1794 by LAURIE & WHIT

Admission ticket for Vauxhall Gardens

This admission ticket for Ranelagh Gardens' rival venue shows Orpheus, a legendary character in ancient Greek religion and mythology, wearing laurel wreath and playing the lyre. He is pictured with a giraffe, bear, rabbit, dog and ape playing the violin. The token is pierced for suspension.

ENGRAVED AND RELIEF
CARVED SILVER, 1751
H. 4 cm. British Museum, MG.684,
donated by Montague Guest.

VIEW IN THE ZOOLOGICAL GARDENS, REGENTS PARK LONDON.

SUMMER FASHIONS for 1837, by B. READ, & H. BODMAN, 12, Hart St. Bloomsbury Sqr. & 95, Str.

also Broad Way New York AMERICA.

View in the Zoological Gardens, Regent's Park

London Zoo was opened to the public in 1828. The elephant and giraffes shown in this view arrived in 1834 and 1836 respectively, joining a collection of animals including kangaroos, llamas and zebras. This advertisement, however, is more about the fashionably dressed visitors than the animals, who paraded through the gardens, displaying their expensive attire and well-dressed children.

COLOUR AQUATINT AND
ETCHING, 1837, BY AN
ANONYMOUS ARTIST
43.1 x 58.3 cm. British Museum,
1937,1102.8.

Ice skating

Ice skating was a popular winter activity, and the Serpentine in Hyde Park would freeze over frequently enough to enable Londoners to become accustomed to the event. That said, skating is a difficult skill to perfect, and crowded ice inevitably caused stumbles, providing an amusing subject for printmakers.

BRUSH DRAWING IN GREY
WASH, WITH WATERCOLOUR
AND GRAPHITE, *c*.1750,
BY SAMUEL HIERONYMUS
GRIMM (1733–1794)

14.1 x 19.9 cm. British Museum,
1931,1114.121, donated by
F. Laura Cannan.

Traffic and transport

A CITY AS LARGE AS LONDON has always depended on transport to function. The Great Fire of London in 1666 offered the perfect opportunity to rebuild the medieval city in a practical, grid layout, but despite the many plans submitted, it was a haphazard and unplanned city that emerged from the ashes. As London's population swelled, the streets clogged, bridges groaned, and ferries heaved with the pressure of transporting people. Like many of the less attractive aspects of the city, topographers often ignored the traffic, choosing instead to present a sedate city with busy yet ordered street scenes. Satirists by contrast revelled in the chaos, and wood-engravers working for illustrated newspapers would on occasion give a more realistic impression of London's traffic woes.

Miseries of London

In this humorous print, Rowlandson satirizes
the troubles caused by traffic on London's narrow
city streets. Here, horse-drawn carriages and
coaches clash, clogging up the road and causing
consternation on all sides. Street traders on the
corner are knocked over and road rage riles up
passengers, who attack each other with whips.
While Rowlandson exaggerates the problem for
satirical effect, traffic has been a real difficulty
for London since the nineteenth century, and
continues to enrage Londoners today.

HAND-COLOURED ETCHING
WITH STIPPLE, 1807, BY
THOMAS ROWLANDSON
(1756–1827)

27.5 x 37.1 cm. British Museum,
1947,1215.1.

MISERIES OF LONDON.

...rage delayed by a jam of coaches — which choak up the whole street, and allow you at...
...our wits for table talk —

...st against breast with ruinous afsault.

...deafning shock, they come —

Pub.d Feb.y 1.st 1807 by R. Ackerman N.o 101 Strand

Cheapside – the Wood Paving Removed

This wood-engraving shows the impact of construction work on the traffic down Cheapside, a major city thoroughfare. A more balanced view than Rowlandson's *Miseries of London* (see p. 72), it still gives the impression of a never ending mass of people and vehicles.

WOOD ENGRAVING WITH LETTERPRESS, 1846, BY AN ANONYMOUS ARTIST
16.1 x 23.2 cm. British Museum, 1880,1113.3549.

Hyde Park Corner

This print shows that Hyde Park Corner was a traffic hotspot even in 1842, as the stout couple in the foreground are hurried angrily across the road by aggressive men on horseback and carriage drivers brandishing whips.

LITHOGRAPH, 1842, BY AN ANONYMOUS ARTIST

19.5 x 30.2 cm. British Museum, 1880,1113.1892.

The Royal Mails at the Angel Inn Islington

This view shows Royal Mail coaches outside the Angel Inn in Islington on the birthday of George IV. The king's birthday occasioned an annual procession by the Royal Mail, and here we see the coaches at night, preparing to depart around the country. In the early nineteenth century much investment was put into improving roads and engineering faster coaches, but journeys remained prohibitively long for many. The advent of the railway in Queen Victoria's reign (1837–1901) brought an end to the long distance coach journey.

HAND-COLOURED AQUATINT, 1828–30,
BY RICHARD GILSON REEVE (1803–1809),
AFTER JAMES POLLARD (1792–1867)
53.3 x 73.8 cm. British Museum, 1880,1113.4908.

The Station at Euston Square

Here we see an early passenger train, with open top carriages
full of people waiting to depart. Euston Station opened in 1837,
the first of London's mainline stations, serving the London and
Birmingham Railway. Two stationary steam engines worked the
ropes that brought the trains in and out of the station, as each
train engine was detached and reattached at Camden.

HAND-COLOURED ETCHING
AND AQUATINT, 1837,
BY JOHN HARRIS (THE
YOUNGER, 1791–1873),
AFTER THOMAS TALBOT
BURY (1811–77)
24.2 x 28.6 cm. British Museum,
1880,1113.4743.

Southwark Bridge from London Bridge

The River Thames was used as a thoroughfare far more commonly in earlier centuries than today. Small rowing boats, barges and later steamships littered the river, transporting people across the capital. From 1555, The Company of Watermen controlled the business of ferrying people around the city, and they continue to work on the River Thames today.

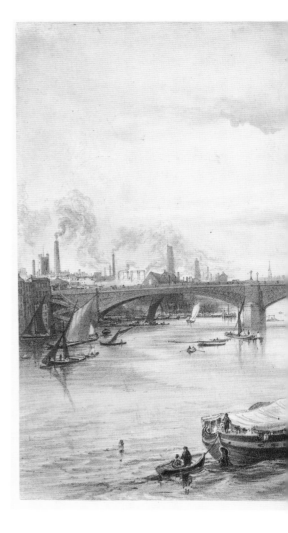

Ferry ticket

BRASS TICKET ISSUED BY
THE STEAM BOAT COMPANY,
19TH CENTURY

Diam. 4.3 cm. British Museum, J.2951.

WILLIAM PARROTT

HAND-COLOURED LITHOGRAPH, 1841,
BY WILLIAM PARROTT (1813–69)

22.3 x 41 cm. British Museum, 1948,0315.1.55,

bequeathed by Hermann Marx.

St Paul's from Ludgate Hill

Boys' energetic view of a busy but moving Ludgate Hill forms part of a larger series of London street views, each introducing the realities of street life without letting them impose on the essential grandeur of the city. Pedestrians stroll unharried, despite their close proximity to the vehicles winding their way along the narrow street. The strongest impression comes from the tall buildings and spire of St Martin's, framing St Paul's.

LITHOGRAPH WITH TINT STONE AND HAND-COLOURING, 1842, BY THOMAS SHOTTER BOYS (1803–74).
43.8 x 31.2 cm. British Museum, 1948,0315.10.21, bequeathed by Hermann Marx.

Temple Bar

The forced narrowing of the road between Fleet Street and the Strand at Temple Bar caused continual traffic problems for London until the removal of the arch in 1878. Malton's sedate view tells us nothing of these traffic woes, instead choosing to present a near empty street, with elegantly dressed pedestrians keeping to the pavements. It is a good example of the sort of artistic license topographers often brought to views of London's busy streets in the eighteenth century.

ETCHING AND HAND-COLOURING, 1796, BY THOMAS MALTON (1748–1804)

21.2 x 29.7 cm. British Museum, G,6.162, bequeathed by John Charles Crowle.

Construction

CONSTRUCTION IS AT THE HEART of a city's prosperity. While today London's road users may wilt at the sight of flashing lights and a line of orange cones, in the past these works brought sewers and paving, heralding great improvements to the everyday life of Londoners. Exceptional feats of engineering, such as the construction of bridges and tunnels, improved both London's infrastructure, and its grandeur. As the industrial revolution took hold, construction projects gained steam, pushing the city to its limits, creating, by 1851, 'the metropolis of the civilized world' (Thorold, 1999). However, the act of building was not a popular subject for artists, who preferred to celebrate the finished product. That said, there were those who recorded construction, and their work gives an intriguing glimpse of the extraordinary manpower and engineering prowess needed to create a city as magnificent as London.

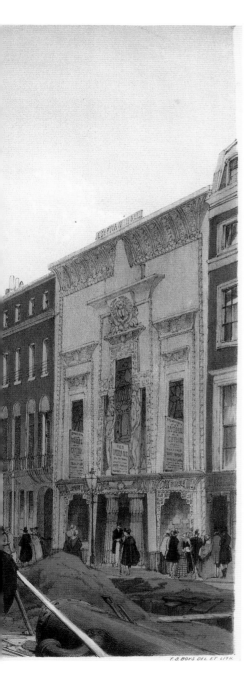

T.S. BOYS DEL. ET LITH.

Piccadilly looking towards the City

Boys was an artist happy to include scenes of construction in his views of London. Here we have a view of Piccadilly from the end of Old Bond Street; Burlington House and Fortnum and Mason's are among prominent buildings on the street. The foreground, however, is dominated by construction, as workmen laying drains dig up the centre of the street. Londoners appear unperturbed by the work, continuing with their business, and pointing up to the hot air balloons sailing over the scene.

HAND-COLOURED
LITHOGRAPH, 1842,
BY THOMAS SHOTTER
BOYS (1803–74)
32 x 43.2 cm. British Museum,
1948,0315.4.77, bequeathed by
Hermann Marx.

The Old and New London-Bridges

taken from the steps at the City end (looking south)
during the progress of the works, August 27, 1830

Work began on the new London Bridge in 1823.
While the new bridge was under construction,
the old bridge continued to be used, as can be
seen in this view. In the foreground a workman
relaxes next to a stone at least twice his size,
illustrating the scale of the construction project.
Cooke was one of a number of artists who
recorded the construction and demolition
of the new and old London Bridges.

ETCHING, 1832, BY EDWARD
WILLIAM COOKE (1811–80)
28.5 x 34.9 cm. British Museum,
1880,1113.1581.

An Elevated View of the New Dock in Wapping

William Daniell's extraordinary series of views of London Docks was made while the docks were still under construction. The long inscription below tells us much about London's pretensions at the turn of the century:

This view represents the first part of the Works, as they will appear when finished, which are now executing in Wapping near the Tower, by the patriotic exertions of the London Dock Company, for the improvement of the Port of London. The bason which is here shewn is 1260 feet in length & 690 feet in breadth, containing an Area of 20 Acres, and its object is the accommodation of vessels employed in every branch of Commerce, for which extensive ranges of appropriate Warehouses are preparing within the enclosure. This great public work is conceived on the scale calculated to support the dignity of the Nation, and the important interests of its Commerce, and will, when compleated, in conjunction with other magnificent works, either in progress or contemplation, render this Metropolis ultimately the first Port, as it is already the first City in the World.

HAND-COLOURED SOFT-GROUND
ETCHING AND AQUATINT, 1803,
BY WILLIAM DANIELL (1769–1837)

47.1 x 78.8 cm. British Museum, G,13.19, bequeathed
by John Charles Crowle (from the Crowle Pennant).

Construction of London Bridge

The drawing above shows the new London Bridge at an early stage of construction, seen from the south, looking towards St Paul's. Only three pontoons are in place at this stage, and the process of laying the arches can be seen. In the background is Southwark Bridge, opened in 1819.

PEN AND BROWN INK WITH
WATERCOLOUR, 1826, WILLIAM
HENRY KEARNEY (1800–58)
21.5 x 47.4 cm. British Museum, 1940,0429.2.

At the British Museum

One of the large iron girders used in the construction of the Lycian Room of the British Museum is here shown after crashing to the floor, trapping a workman. The dangers of large scale architectural projects are here highlighted by Scharf, as the grand pretensions of the city required ever more challenging feats of engineering and construction. This sketch shows a side of London's expansion rarely documented.

GRAPHITE DRAWING, 1844,
BY GEORGE SCHARF (1788–1860)
23 x 18.1 cm. British Museum, 1900,0725.30,
bequeathed by Sir George Scharf (artist's son).

Girder is
c
5 Tons. 3060
2 quarter. 16 H

It takes 4 hours
to wind up a Girder
this was five Tons weight
and fell where it was near
the top, it broke into 4 pieces
nearly broke a man's Leg

G. Scharf del.
13 August 1849

Accident of a Rope breaking in hoisting a Girder
at the Building of the Lycian Room at the British Museum

2 y

Sewer works on Fleet Street

Sewers are not an attractive subject, and few images of early sewers were made. This sketch, from the *Illustrated London News* from 1845, is interesting for showing us a cross section of the sewer works on Fleet Street. The depth of the sewer is here revealed, along with the precarious positions of the workmen.

WOOD-ENGRAVING, 1845,
BY AN ANONYMOUS ARTIST

18.7 x 10.5 cm. British Museum,
1880,1113.3157.2.

Sewer works on Fleet Street

This sketch is taken from the same paper as the previous, this time recording the inconvenience caused by such deep sewer works. The construction works in conjunction with the narrowing of the road at Temple Bar must have made the road close to impassable at busy times. The lack of safety equipment for the men working deep in the trench is also evident.

WOOD-ENGRAVING, 1845,
BY AN ANONYMOUS ARTIST
14.5 x 14.8 cm. British Museum,
1880,1113.3157.1.

Fire, crime and punishment

AS A GENRE, TOPOGRAPHY TENDS TO BE BLIND to the darker, more unpleasant sides of life. The exception is fire, an event so dramatic and devastating it is not surprising many artists chose to record it. The Great Fire of 1666 was thankfully never to be matched for scale, but many well-known buildings suffered at the hands of fire, including the Royal Exchange (1838) and the Houses of Parliament (1834). In terms of crime and punishment, common criminals were of little interest, but sensational occurrences such as high profile murders, or the capture of notorious highwaymen, would find their way into London's visual history, though often only distributed locally. Punishment, on the other hand, was a more popular subject, with prisons, pillories and executions all finding their place in the picturing of the city. The everyday dreariness of bad weather, dirt and rubbish, is for the most part left to our imaginations.

London im Brand.
Umbständiger Bericht, und
Erschröckliche Fewers-Brunst...

This is an example of one of many broadsides issued on the continent on the Great Fire of London. The long view from the south was a common type, much copied in Germany and the Netherlands, and printmakers simply added flames to the city when news of the fire spread. This German example has clearly been copied from sources themselves quite distant from the city, as it has included a fictitious bend in the River Thames – a common mistake indicating the widespread practice of making views from prints rather than first hand.

ETCHING, 1666, NUREMBERG,
BY CHRISTOPH LOCHNER
THE YOUNGER (1603–77)

14.8 x 36.9 cm (artwork only)

British Museum, 1880,1113.1158.

LONDON im Brand.

SEP.
OCC. OR.
MER.

...ESIS FLUVIUS.

ner war alles umbsonst/ Dann der Wind von Nord-Ost lange
../und widerumb/ als das Fewer am End der Statt gewesi/
esi/in die Statt getrieben/daß also am Montag/ als dritter
../ die Statt vollkommen in Fewer stunde/diß betrifft nur
../ und Handelsleute/so in der Grace-Kirch-Strassen und an
bey der Canon-Strassen wohneten/ Dienstags den 4. Septem
../ die ansehnliche Börse/ (alwo die Kauffleut zusammen
../) In der Nacht verfiel auch die Fleish-Strasse biß an S. Dun
../che/mit allen an der Börse ligenden Plätzen/wie auch das ver
../ von der Tempel Krone Office/ dahmalen stehen die Leut die ver
../ über 8.oder 10.Häuser/aber es wurde doch alles dem Brand
../ welcher seine Sach vor die Statt gebracht/der hat es erhalten/
../ leich 50 Gulden für ein Wagen oder Karren gegeben/so wa
../ wenig zu bekommen/Es liessen Ihro Kön: M. arst. auch disen
../ mittag solche verbieten/in meynung es wurde besser Lüffte ge
../ solches halff doch wenig/worauff Ihro Königl: Maysi: sich
../ resolvierte/etliche Häuser mit Pulffer springen zu lassen/umb
../ dardurch abzuschneiden/welches endlich auch gestiftet/dann
../ an Mittwoch weiter nicht gefressen/ etwelen selbiger biß
../ogs gewähret/und ist damit der Fewer/woran allbereit das
../randt/noch salviert worden. Den eingelangten Bericht noch/
../ auff 12000. Häuser 84. Kirchen/ worunter das
../Gebäu S. Pauli Kirchen/auch mit begriffen. Viel haben ih
../Sachen in die Kirchen geflehnet/ aber alles gieng mit im Fewr
../ey wehrendem Brandt/durfften sich die Teutschen (Holländer)

und Frenkosen wenig sehen lassen/ dann sie übel geschlagen/oder gar
getragen geseht worden. Ein tertlicher Becker in Wesin er isi ist/als
sein Ofen rauchte/ von dem Rolk überfallen/und soll todt geschlagen
worden/doch wehrte Hertzog Jork nach ab; Ein arme Frauen Mor-
feld/ ihrg Reich all exi unter ihren Schwein ersticken zu Stu-
cken gehauen/weil die Leute meinten/man wolte ihnen weiter Fewer
einlegen/wie man sagt selten Gezelt auffgeschlagen werden. Dann die
Versiädt alle gesteckt voller Menschen seynd/ und die Häuser so bald
nicht weider auffgebauet werden können/biß das Modell/ welches das
Parlement entwerffen wird/heraus kommen thut/weil die Kauff und
Handelsleute/ nicht mehr an ihrer gewöhnlichen Ort zusamm kommen
können/ als haben Ihre Königl: Maysi: ihnen den Platz in dem Graf
hon sichen Collegio erlaubt/ihre Versammlung zu halten.

P.S. Es kompt Bericht auß Lenden/ daß viel tausend unschul-
dige Kinder mit einer unglaublichen Meng köstlicher Mobilien/verbron-
nen. Die Teutsche Kirch ist wunderbarlicher weiß/ da doch alle umblig-
gende Häuser abgebrandt/stehen geblieben. Weilen nun nichts als lau-
ter Wehklagen/unter den armen Leuten gehört wird/ Als haben Ihre
Kön: Maysi: alles zuergebachne Brod (so auff die Flott: der Soldatesca
gehörig) unter die Abgebrandte auftheilen lassen/welche sich in die hun-
dert tausend starck vor die Statt ins Feld gelägert haben. Dieses ist nun
geehrter Leser/ dieser großmächtig: und erbärmlichen Fewerbrunst/or-
dentlicher Erzehl: und Beschreibung/ Gott der Allhöchste/ wolle alle
und jede/ vor solchem Unglück Vätterlich behüten.

A M E N.

Fire in London

The Albion Mills were established in 1786, one of the first great steam powered factories in London. Standing on the River Thames next to Blackfriars Bridge, the mills were a wonder to some, but a cause of resentment to mill workers, who saw their livelihood threatened by the new machinery. The fire that broke out in 1791 quickly destroyed the factory, drawing in a large crowd, some of whom celebrated its demise. This print shows firefighters desperately trying to control the flames that billowed over the city.

ETCHING, AQUATINT AND HAND-COLOURING, 1808, BY JOHN BLUCK (*c.*1791–1832 *fl.*), AFTER AUGUSTUS CHARLES PUGIN (1768/69–1832) AND THOMAS ROWLANDSON (1756–1827)
21.5 x 26.3 cm. British Museum, 1880,1113.1489.

Mr Sheldon's Ballon on Fire

PEN AND INK WITH
WATERCOLOUR, 1784,
BY CHARLES FRANCIS
GREVILLE (1749–1809)
22.4 x 35.8 cm. British Museum,
1880,1113.4515.

The first balloon ascent in England was made in 1784 by Vincenzo Lunardi (1759–1806). The event caused great excitement and encouraged further attempts around the capital. This drawing by Charles Greville records Dr Sheldon's failed attempt to launch a balloon of much greater dimensions than Lunardi's, in the gardens of Foley House, near Regent's Park. The adventure took place just ten days after Lunardi's success, but ended in disaster as the balloon caught fire, and Greville, who was watching from Portland Square, was able to record the epic flop. This is an unusual drawing for showing failure at a time when most artists were celebrating London's success.

The New Sucking Worm Fire Engine

This intriguing print shows John Lofting's design for a fire engine that could carry water over distances through long leather pipes. In the centre is a cross section of a tall building with men fighting the flames at different levels. Outside are two engines, with pipes extending far enough to carry water over the Royal Exchange, and the Monument, erected in memory of the Great Fire of London. The views below show the engine at work on a ship, in a distillery, and in a formal garden.

ETCHING WITH
LETTERPRESS
EXPLANATION,
1668–1720, BY AN
ANONYMOUS ARTIST
46.5 x 53.8 cm. British Museum,
G,10.76, bequeathed by
John Charles Crowle.

The Murder of Thomas Thynne Esq in Pall Mall

Here is an example of a scandalous murder that did attract enough attention to be recorded. Thomas Thynne was a man of status, and his murder in 1682 at the hands of Count Koningsmark, the rejected suitor of Thynne's wife, on Pall Mall, a well-to-do London road, was not an ordinary event. Indeed, it was immortalized in sculpture on Thynne's monument in Westminster Abbey. At trial, Koningsmark was acquitted, but the three men hired in his service were hanged.

ETCHING AND ENGRAVING
(POSSIBLY A BOOK
ILLUSTRATION), *c.*1740,
BY ISAAC BASIRE (1704–68),
AFTER J. NICHOLLS (*c.*1740)
28.6 x 19 cm. British Museum, G,5.199,
bequeathed by John Charles Crowle.

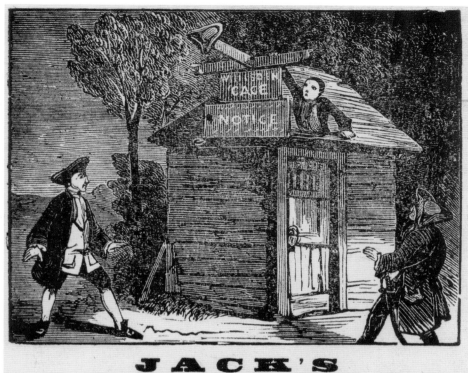

JACK'S ESCAPE FROM WILLESDEN CAGE

Jack's Escape from Willesden Cage

Jack Sheppard was one of London's most notorious criminals. He gained celebrity from his ability to escape confinement. He escaped twice from Newgate Prison before being executed at Tyburn (close to the location of Marble Arch in present-day London). This crude woodcut celebrates Jack's escape from Willesden Cage – a small, confined shed designed to hold petty thieves.

WOODCUT, c.19TH CENTURY, BY AN ANONYMOUS ARTIST

8.4 x 11 cm. British Museum, 1927,1126.1.17.4, bequeathed by George Potter.

HAND-COLOURED ETCHING
AND AQUATINT, 1809, BY
JOHN BLUCK (1791–1832 *fl.*),
AFTER AUGUSTUS CHARLES
PUGIN (1768–1832) AND
THOMAS ROWLANDSON
(1756–1827)
22.2 x 27.3 cm. British Museum,
1880,1113.2238.

Pillory, Charing Cross

The pillory was a form of punishment by public humiliation.
The prisoner would be placed in the pillory in well-known public
locations, and subjected to mocking and jeering from the crowd,
often in addition to the ignominy of being pelted with rubbish.
Here we see two men in the pillory at Charing Cross, overlooked
by the large equestrian statue of Charles I.

Fleet Prison

The Fleet was known as a debtors prison from as early as 1290, and remained in use up until 1846. Notorious for cruelty and squalor, the Fleet Prison was also a destination for secret marriages. The prison was burnt down twice and rebuilt to the same plans, firstly in the Great Fire of 1666, and again in 1780 during the anti-Catholic protest known as the Gordon Riots. This crude drawing shows the raquet ground, with inmates playing against the high wall, beyond which looms the dome of St Paul's.

PEN AND INK WITH
GREY WASH, *c*.1800, BY
AN ANONYMOUS ARTIST
18.8 x 31.4 cm. British Museum,
1916,0524.4, donated by
E. E. Leggatt, Legatt Bros.

Coldbath Fields Prison Gates

In 1794, a 'House of Correction' was built on the site of an old rubbish heap on Coldbath Fields to the north of the city. Rather than being left to fester in their cells, inmates of Coldbath Fields Prison were forced to labour on a treadmill to grind grain and pump water. This drawing by Shepherd shows the intimidating entrance gates to the prison, and the print opposite shows inmates labouring on treadmills of a similar ilk used in Brixton Prison.

WATERCOLOUR, *c*.1850,
BY THOMAS HOSMER
SHEPHERD (1793–1864)
20.5 x 15.9 cm. British Museum,
1880,1113.4848.

ETCHING AND ENGRAVING,
1820–21, BY AN ANONYMOUS
ARTIST

20.8 x 25.5 cm. British Museum,
1872,1214.382.

View of the Treadmill

*for the employment of prisoners, erected at the House of Correction
at Brixton, by Mr Wm Cubitt of Ipswich*

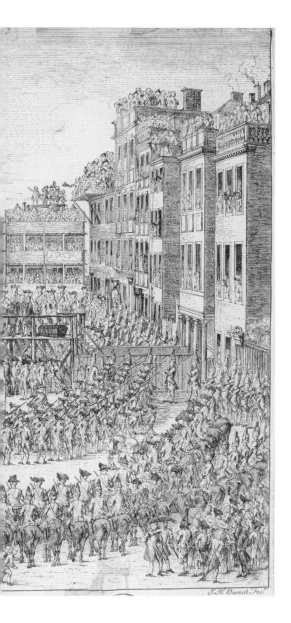

The North West Prospect of the Tower of London

Executions in London were public spectacles, and the trial and execution of Simon Fraser, 11th Lord Lovat, for treason in 1747 engrossed the capital, with many prints made documenting both events. His execution at Tower Hill was the last beheading to take place in London, and temporary scaffolds were erected for the public to watch. In a twist of black humour, one of these scaffolds collapsed killing twenty.

Left ETCHING, 1747, BY J. H. BUNCK (*c.*1750 *fl.*) 34.9 x 48 cm. British Museum, 1880,1113.3458.

Resident's pass

POSSIBLY A PASS ISSUED TO A RESIDENT AT THE TOWER. ENGRAVED WHITE METAL, 1860–79 Diam. 3.2 cm. British Museum, MG.891, donated by Montague Guest.

Further reading

Bernard Adams, 1983, *London Illustrated 1604–1851*, London

Sheila O'Connell (ed.), 2003, *London 1753*, London

H. J. Dyos and Michael Wolff (eds), 1976, *The Victorian City: Images and Realities Volume I*, London

Felicity Myrone, 'The monarch of the plain: Paul Sandby and topography', *in* John Bonehill and Stephen Daniels (eds), 2009, *Paul Sandby: Picturing Britain*, London

Ira Bruce Nadel and F. S. Schwarzbach (eds), 1980, *Victorian Artists and the City: A Collection of Critical Essays*, Oxford

Donald J. Olsen, 1982, *Town Planning in London: The Eighteenth and Nineteenth Centuries*, London and New Haven

J. F. C. Phillips, 1976, *Shepherd's London*, London

Alex Potts, 'Picturing the modern metropolis: images of London in the nineteenth century', in *History Workshop*, No. 26, Winter 1988

Peter Thorold, 1999, *The London Rich: The Creation of a Great City from 1666 to the Present*, London

Malcolm Warner, 1987, *The Image of London: Views by Travellers and Emigres 1550–1920*, London